I0470508

# J U M B l E d :

### artist' view of Parkinson's
Patrick

created by :                     rick B. Humphreys

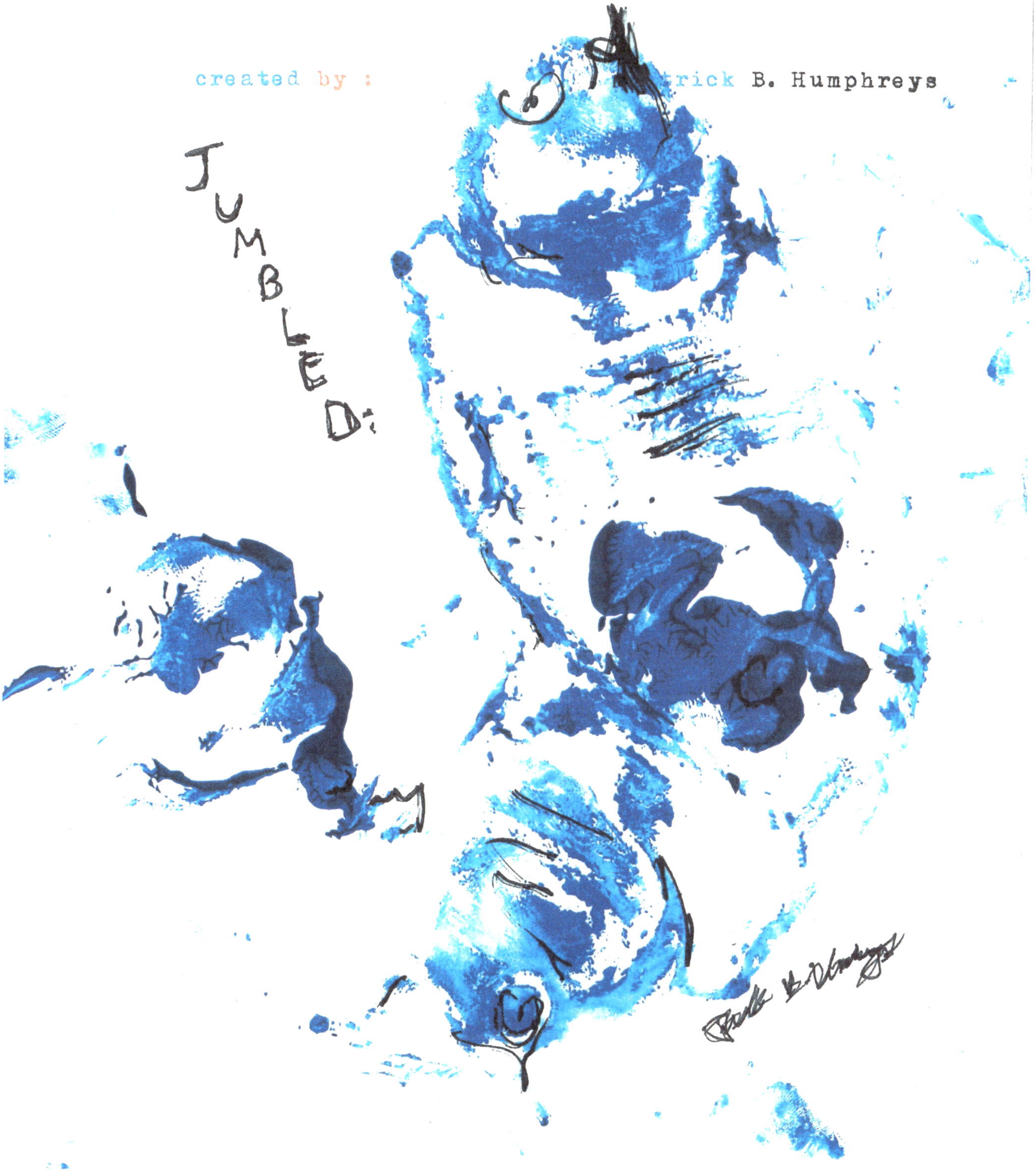

JUMBLED:

I was diagnosed at a young age . I was 41 when    i
fo und out i had parkinson's.

        I am considered young onset. I Want to  live to
very old.  i feel young . young enough to play with teddy
bears .


RED   YELLOW GREEN      teddy bear or gummy bears
to eat    or g e t      e a t e n,  which will it be

YOUNG ONSET.

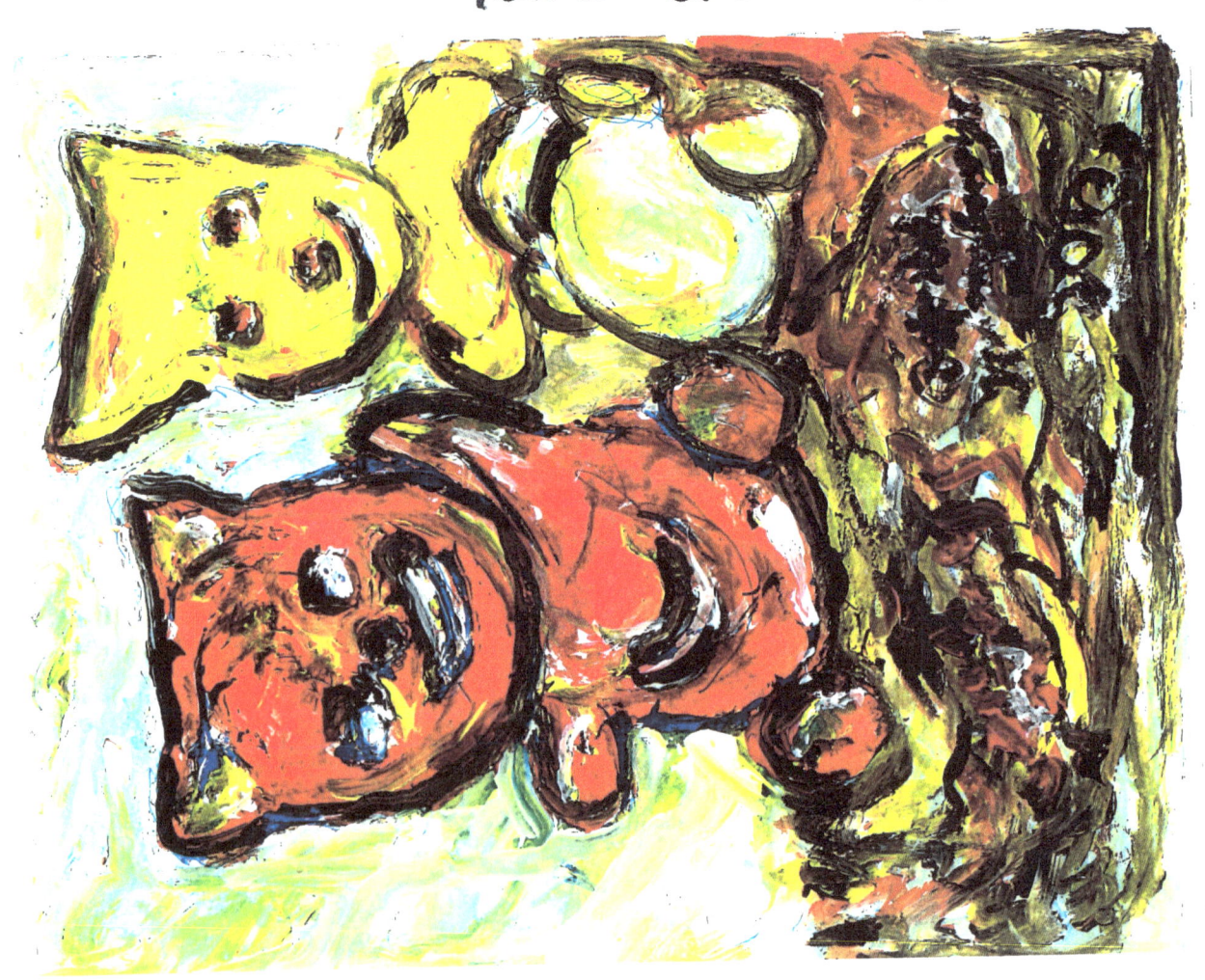

I feel like a puppet with my strings cut.

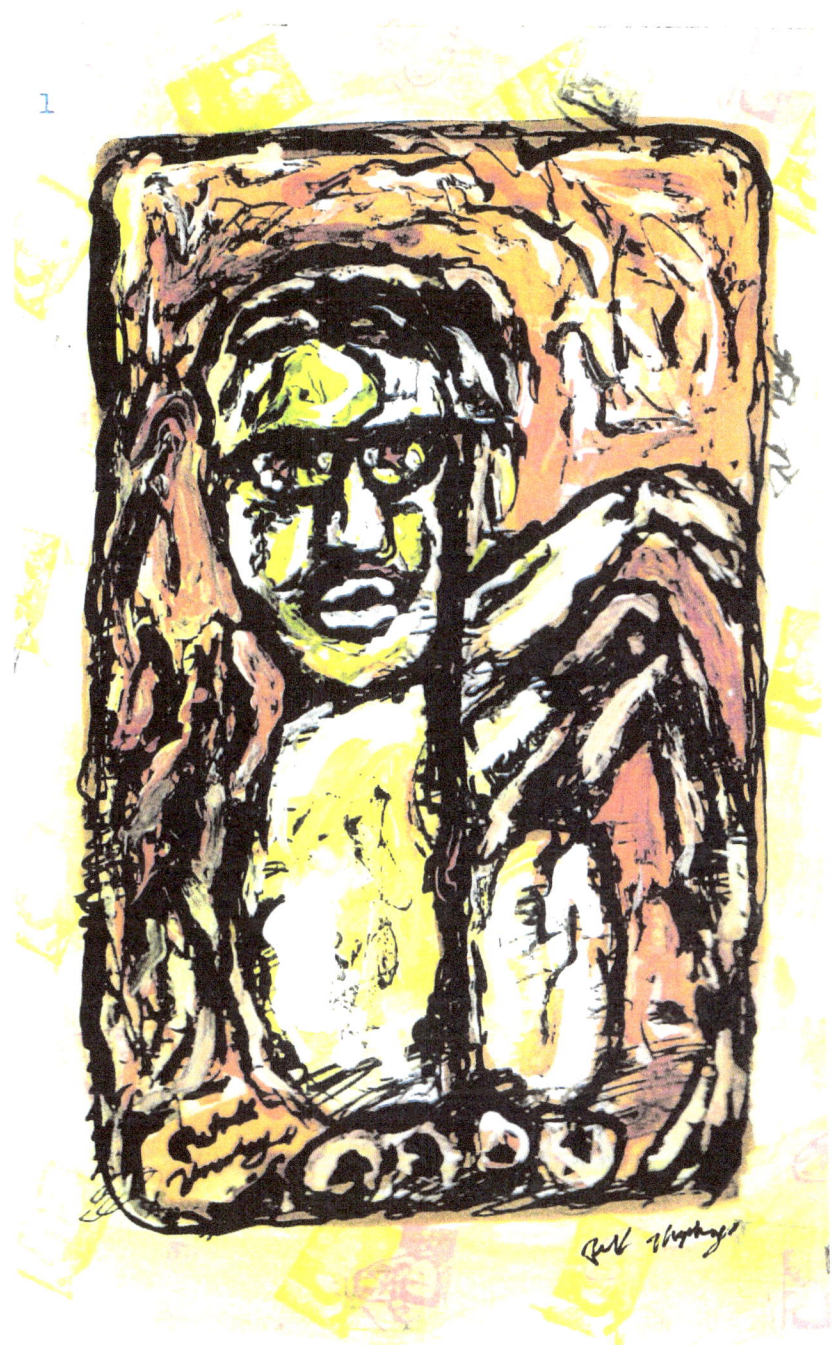

whO is

pulling my

strings

do you feel

like you

lost control

are we ever

in control

please help

SHADOW PUPPET

# FREEzING

Can  NOT move , frozen in spot

frozen in my body , can't move , want to

go away , go close , can you please please

move along,   soapy trails , which

n n nn m   way to go . which way to go?

please body let me, can anybody release
my soul,   like a elephant infant
b  toy that is stuck in gum, frozen to the
DeSk , i don't want to, please don't
this is it,       Freezing

## FREEZING

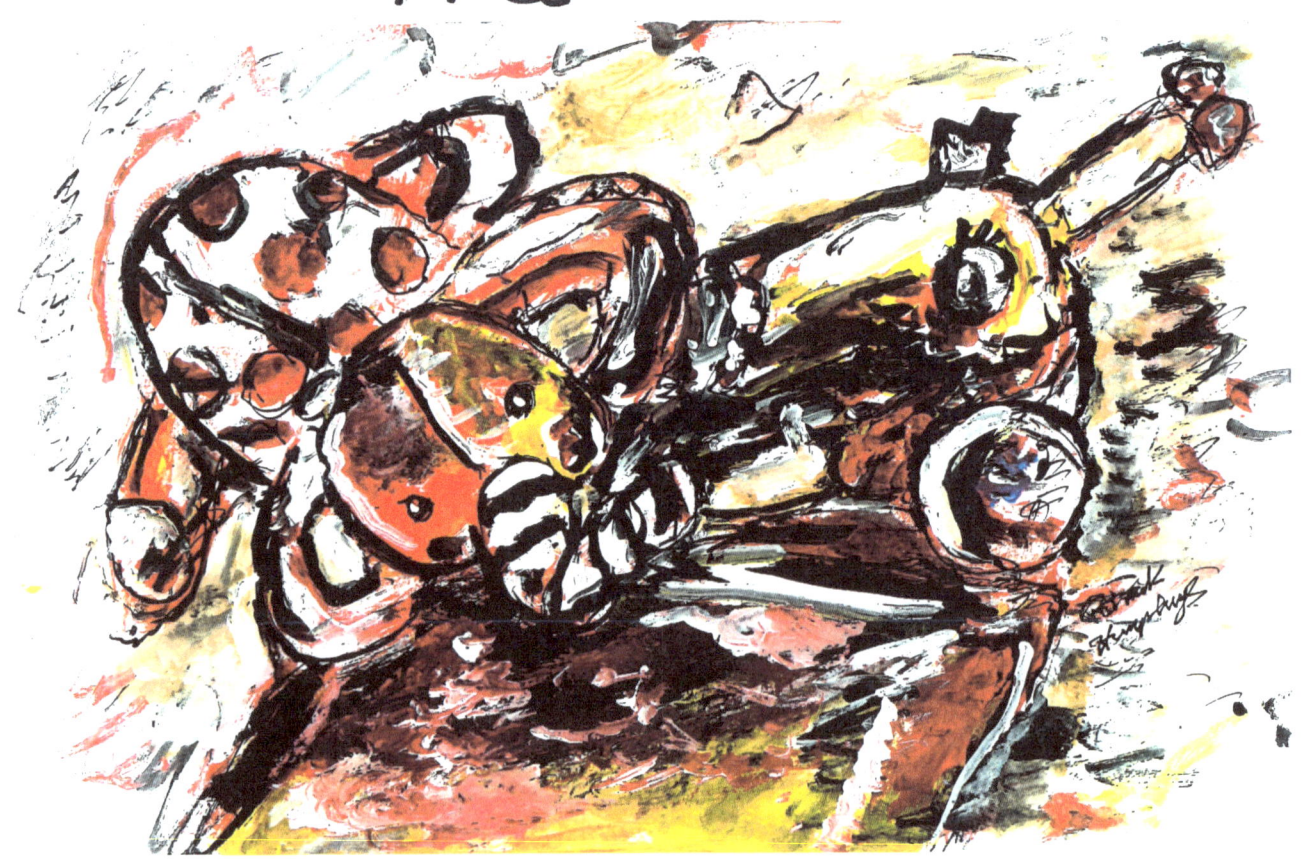

M  a S k like  expression

p oker face can not read emo tion  poker face like

a King playing card          full house two of a kind

DEPRESsioN    ;;;;  $&@

?              '              common to

                                      Parkinson's

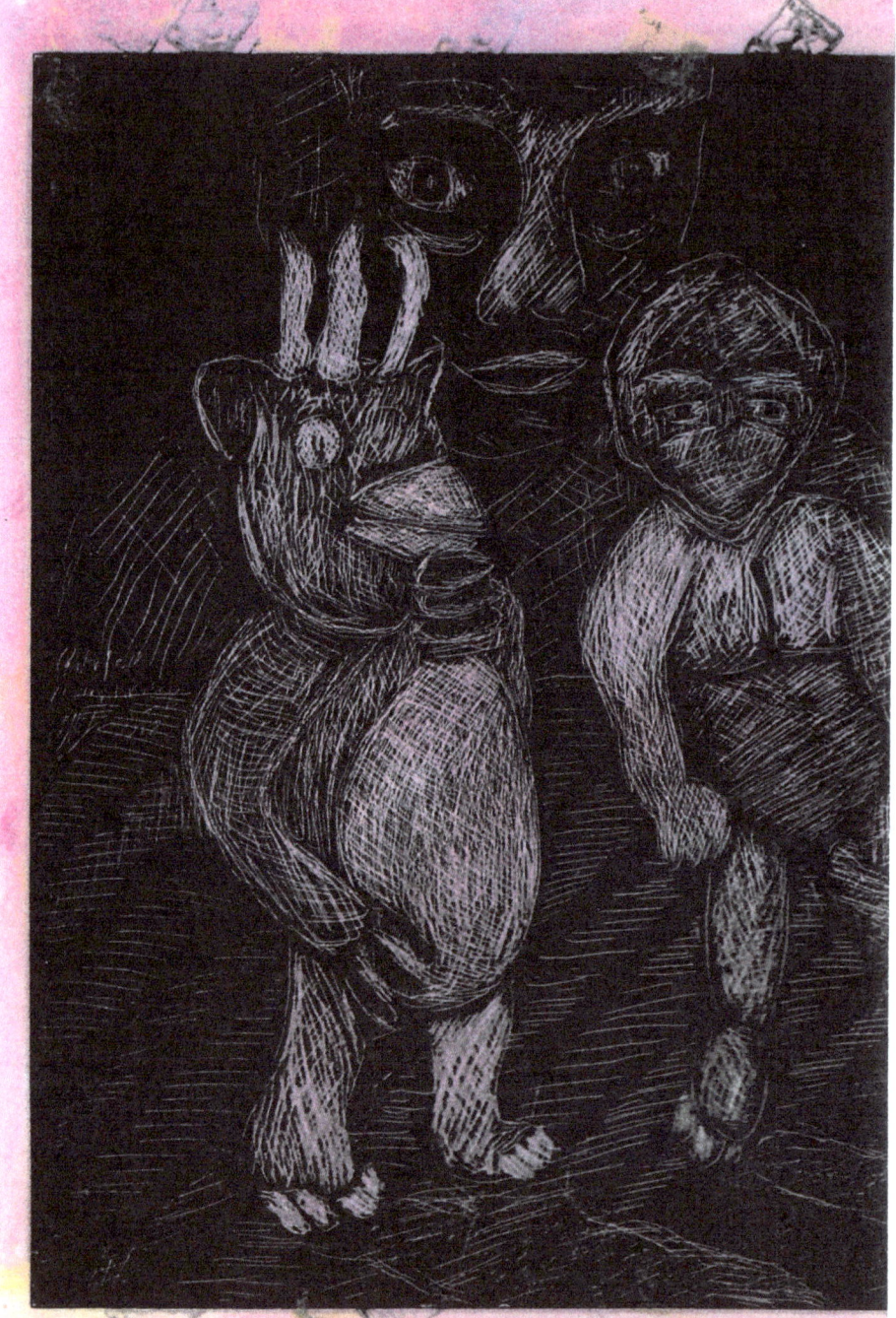

common to

many if

not all
  2 3 $)(!

DEPRESSION ?!#%

i want

i need


to be


there  for

my



son,

Cameron



i want to

need to



i am

your  father



i love

you



i just want to

be i am here

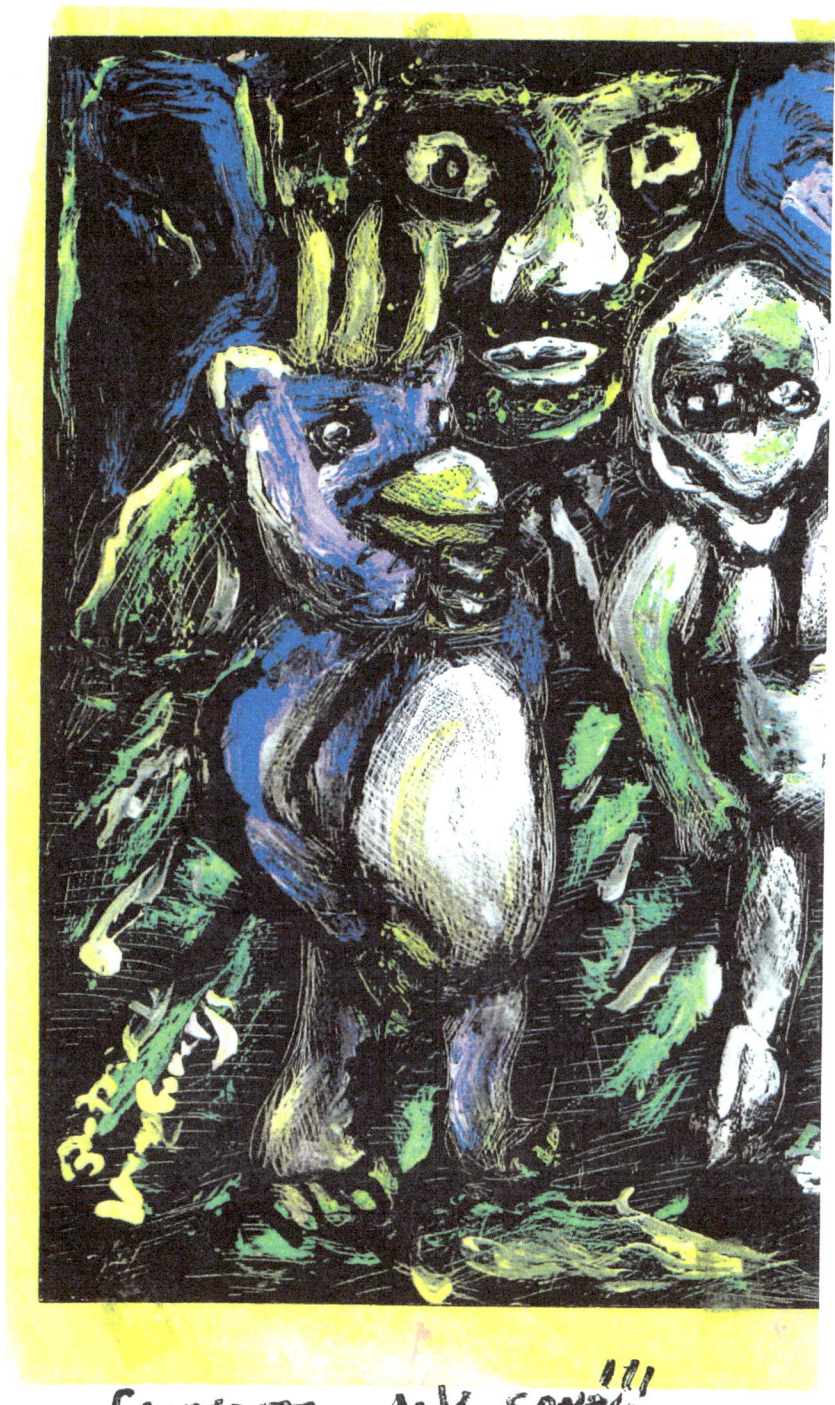

Cameron, MY son!!!

Numerous as fish in the sea:

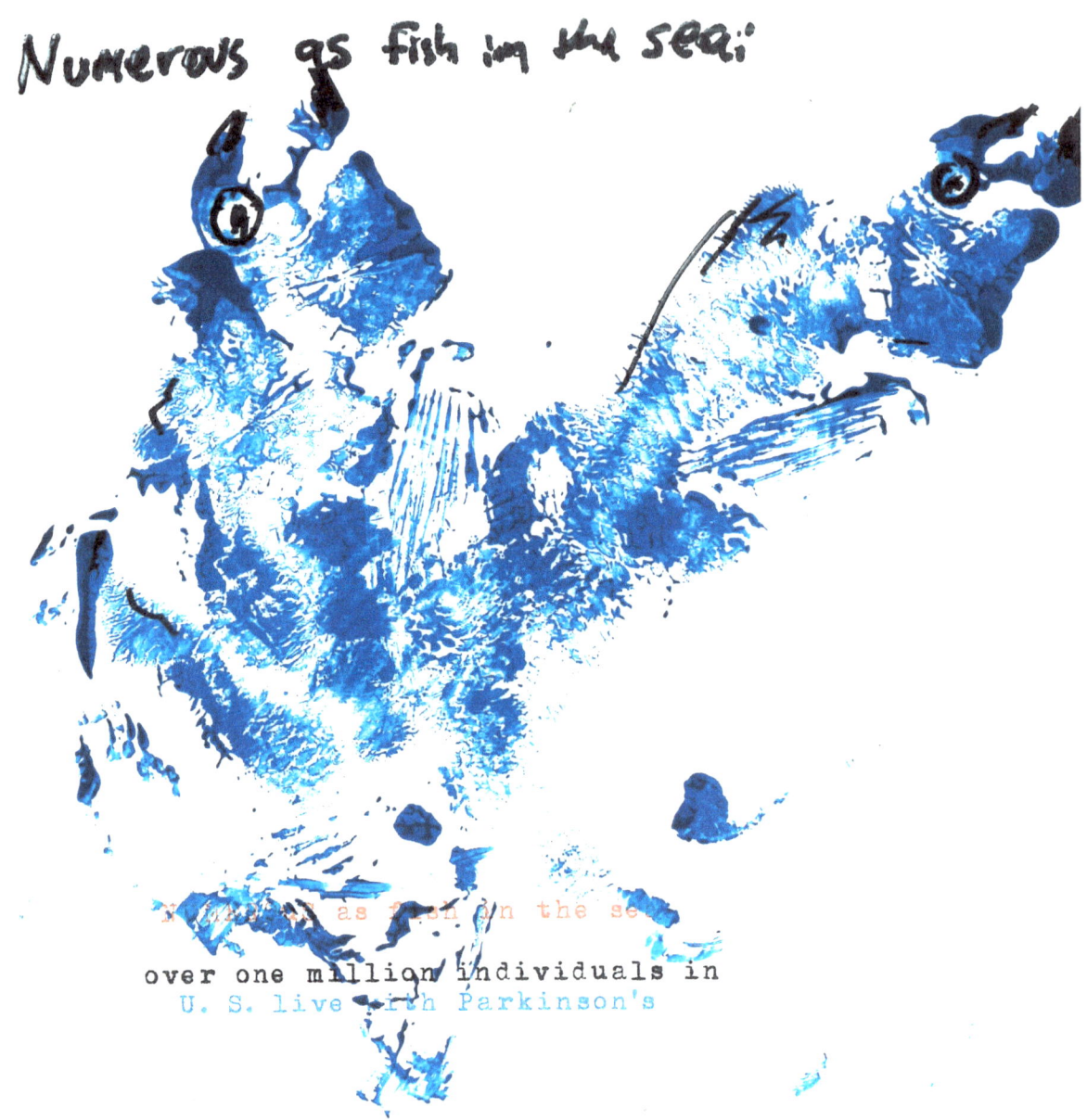

numerous as fish in the sea

over one million individuals in
U. S. live with Parkinson's

4 % are under age of 50

are .called  young onset
i was 41          5 years ago

many more to      go where to go

M I C R O G R A P H I A

b   bbbbbbb       shrinkage in handwriting , keeps
     getting   smaller smaller indeed who does the
                    signature says you  can
                    still stay here
                please close the d o o r

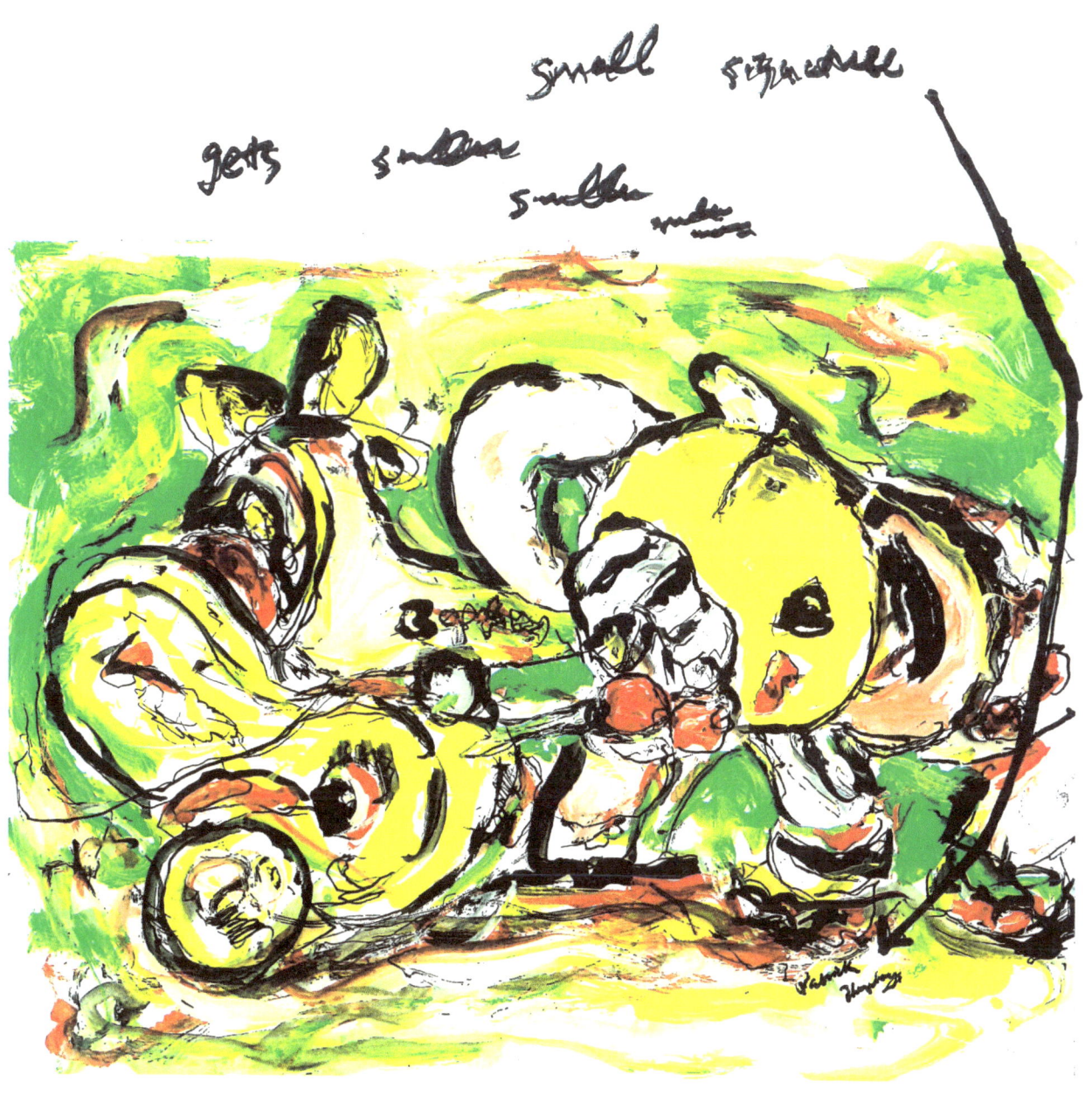

A M I   G O I N G   T O   Die ?

R a n g d a  the   witch    fr om BALI

MYSTICAL          AM I GOING TO DIE ?...

DIE

YES

NO

TRUTH

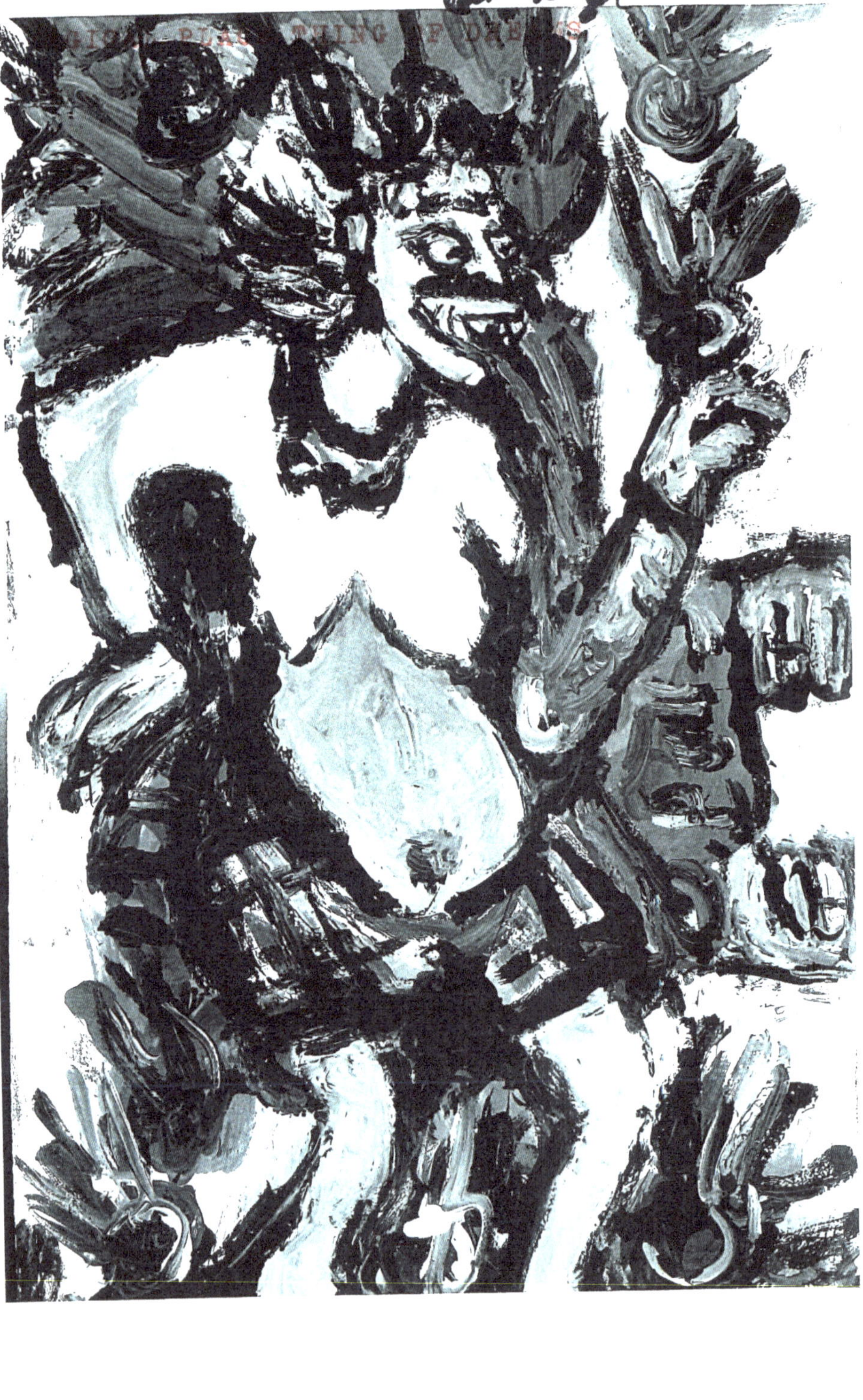

bb    B R A D Y K I N E S I A

slowness of movement.   having Parkinson's

makes you slower , very slow sometimes you

F reeze altogether , feel like a dragon

going through the sky whose breathe whose

fire has gone out ,    Do not lose your fire

fight   the fight , be the dragon , be

my desire ,      a dragon in flight

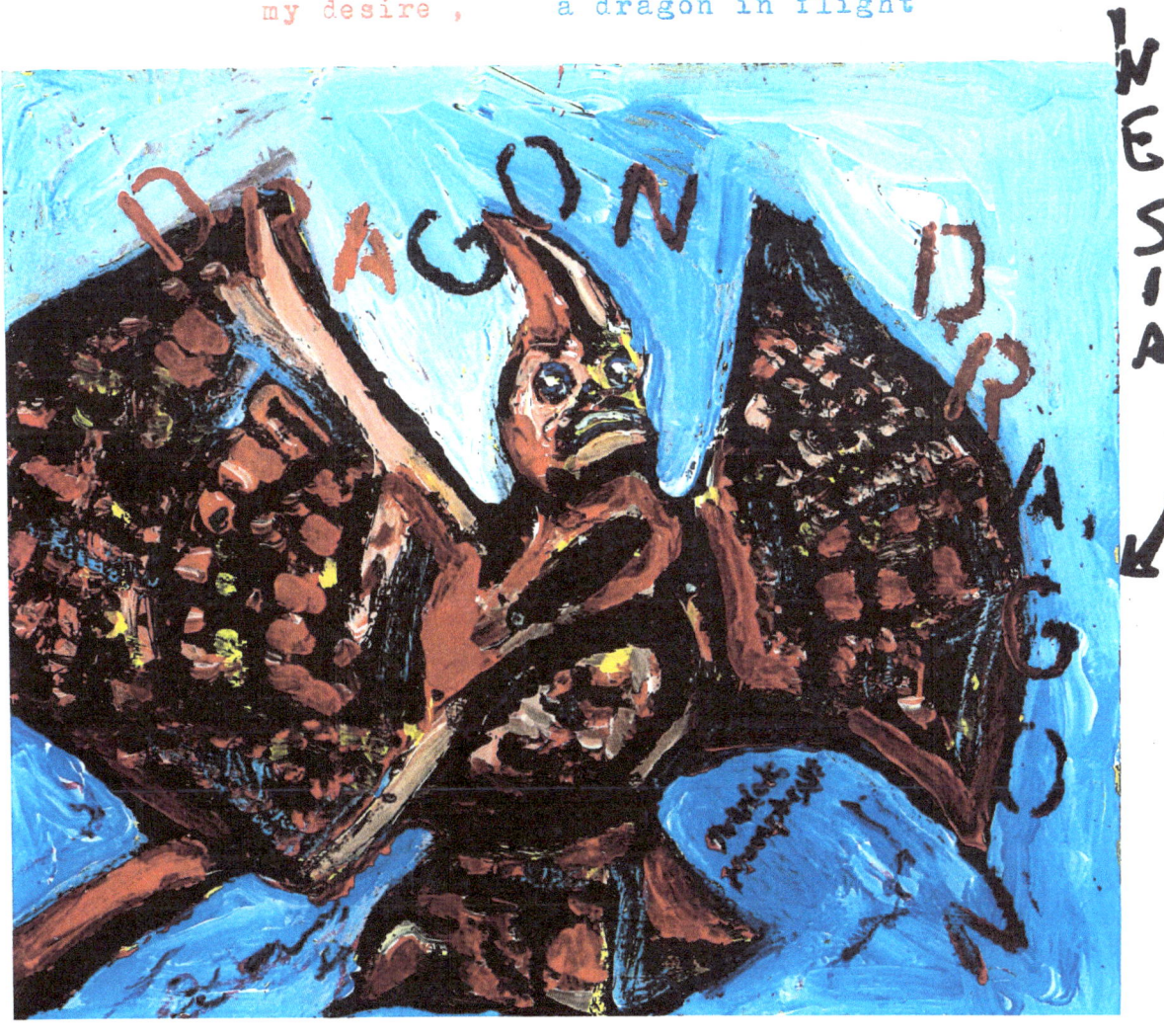

BRADYKINESIA

C O N F usion    i just do not know

alone in a cold house        stay with me

cover me like a warm blanket        please don't

pull up the covers I am confused

CONFUSION

Confusion              Confusion    which

way to go    who answers who    is in control

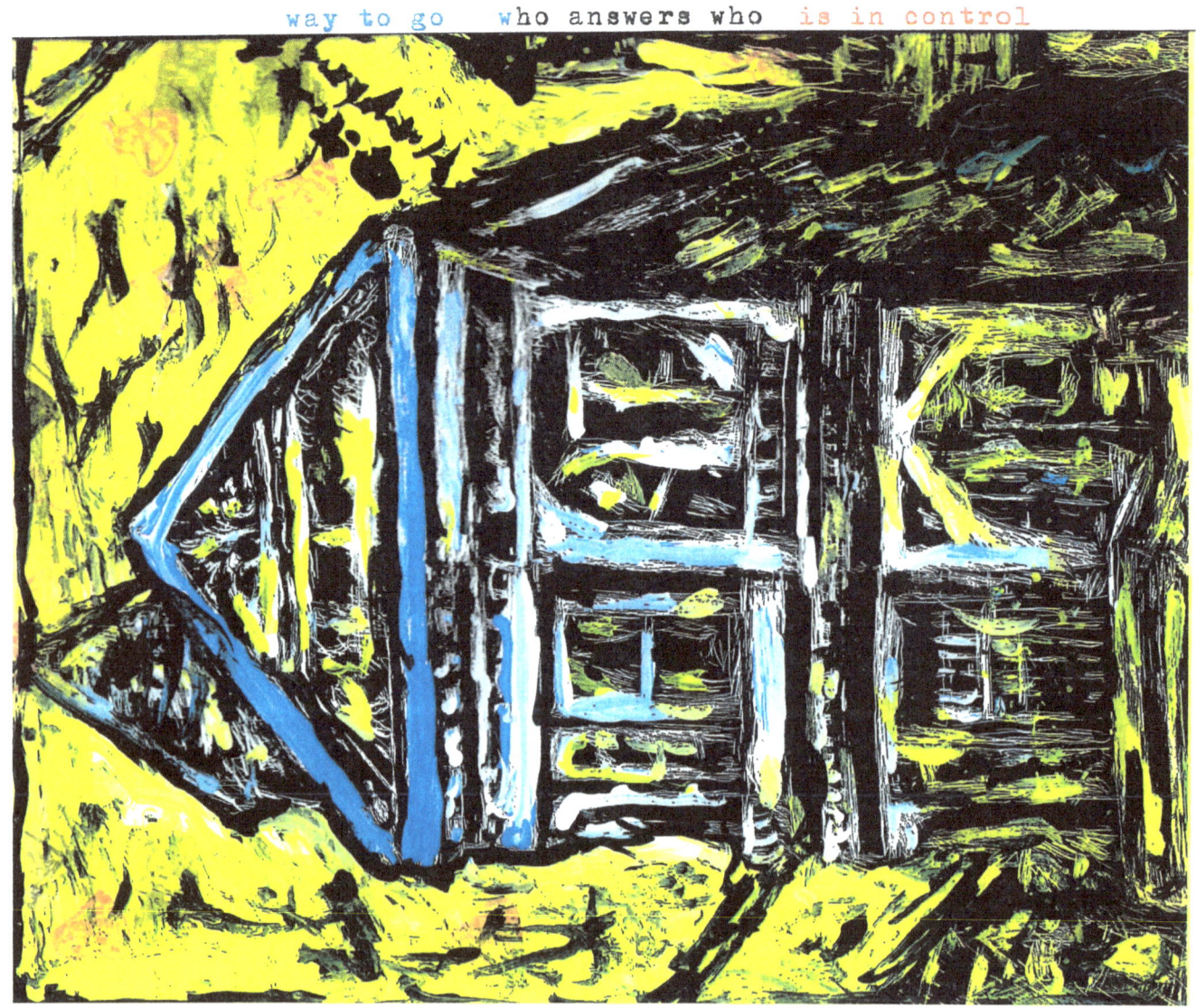

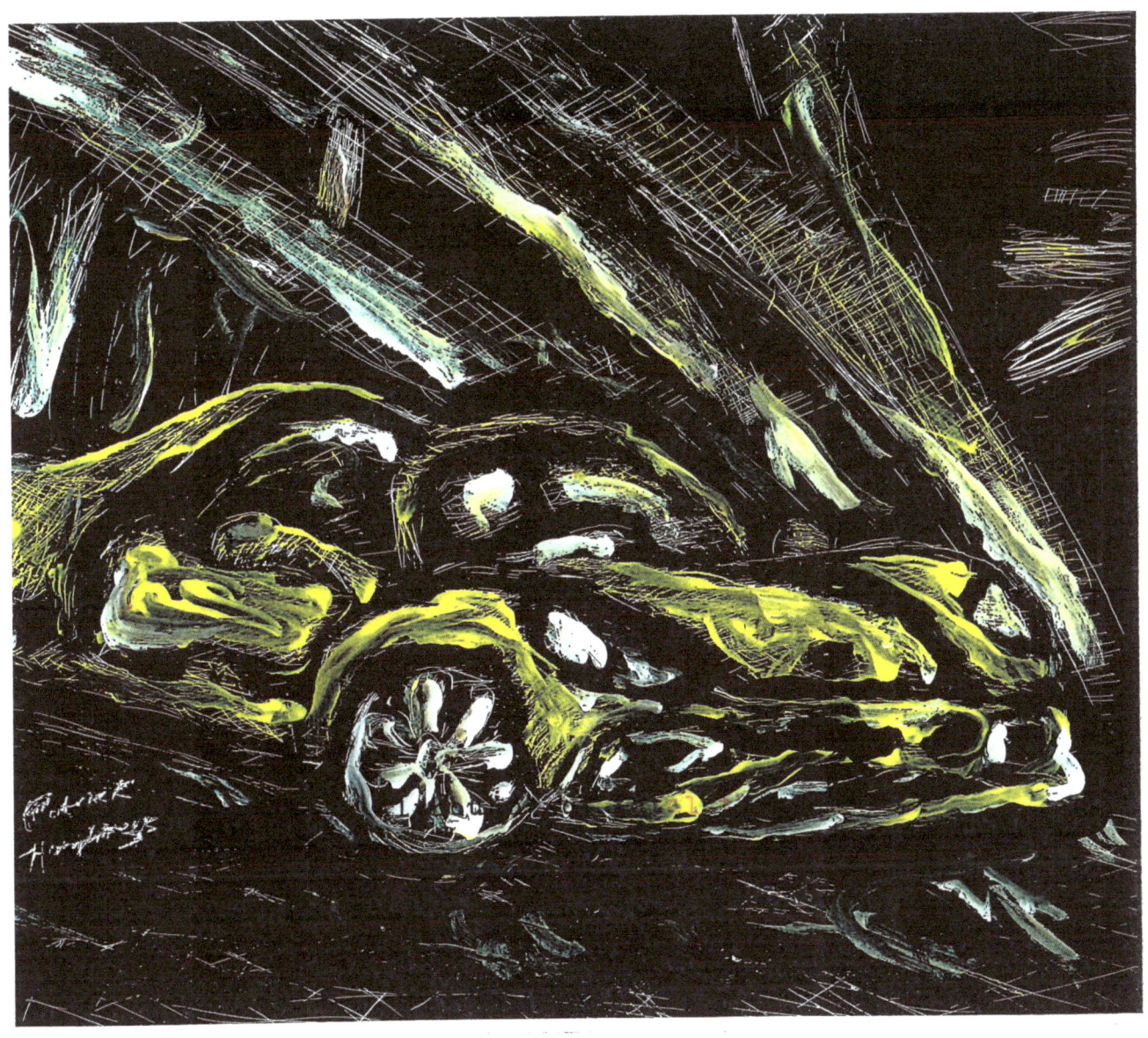

a cure could yes could come like
a fast  very fast curved perfection
motor running tires burning ....
metal emotion vehicle spinning....

Although not Fatal, there is

no cure for Parkinson's

Sometimes i  T R E M O R

like a full B L O W N funny car

wheels turning        tires smokin'

can you control the beast
will the Tremor win or will you ???

FULL BLOWN!!!

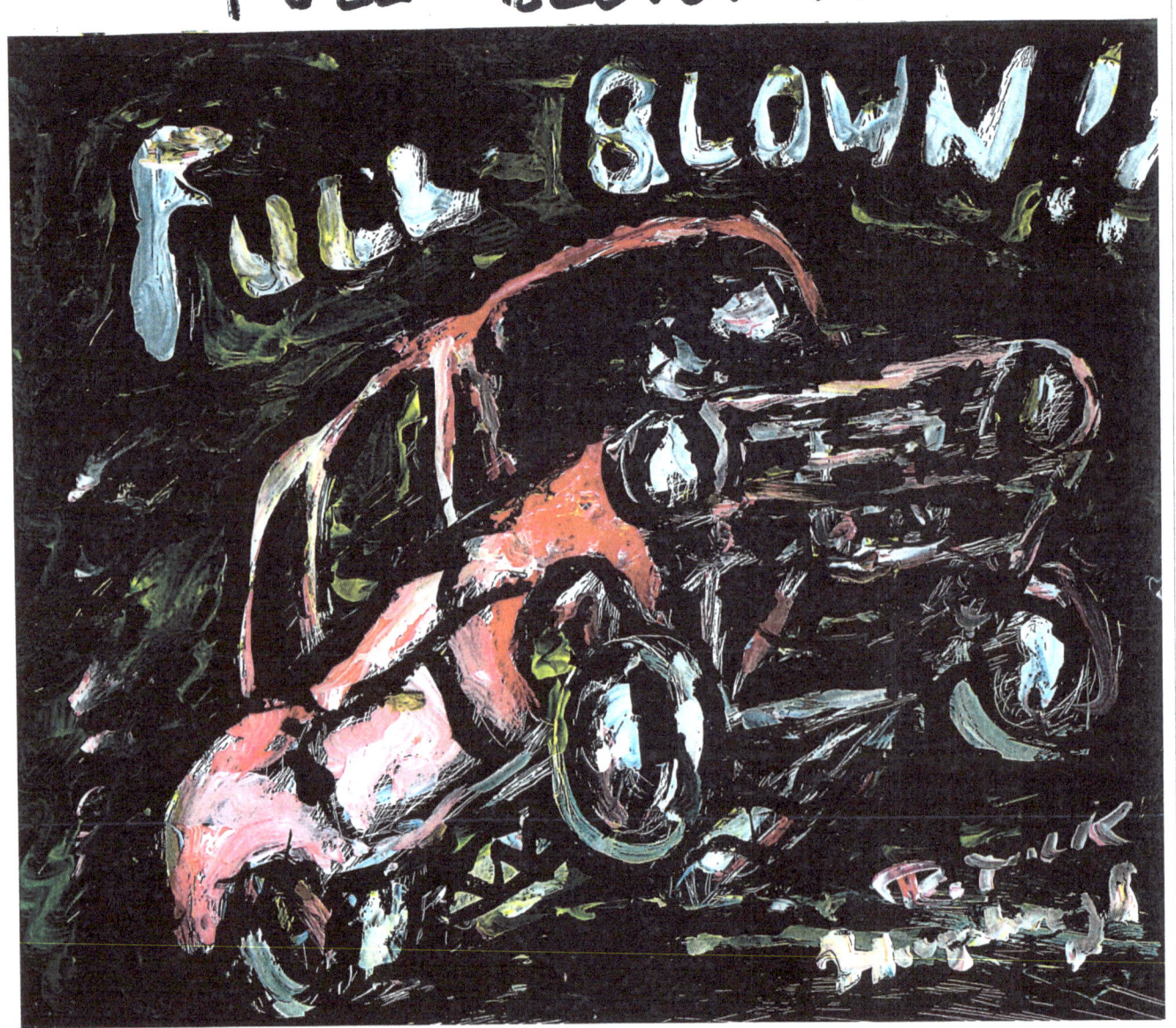

D E M E N T I A : : feel like a chicken

with its head cut off . Many Parkinson's

patients develop signs of dementia  later

in life .

this as well as

other  symptoms

make this a

disease that makes

you feel like a

chicken out of control

don't lose control

do not lose your head

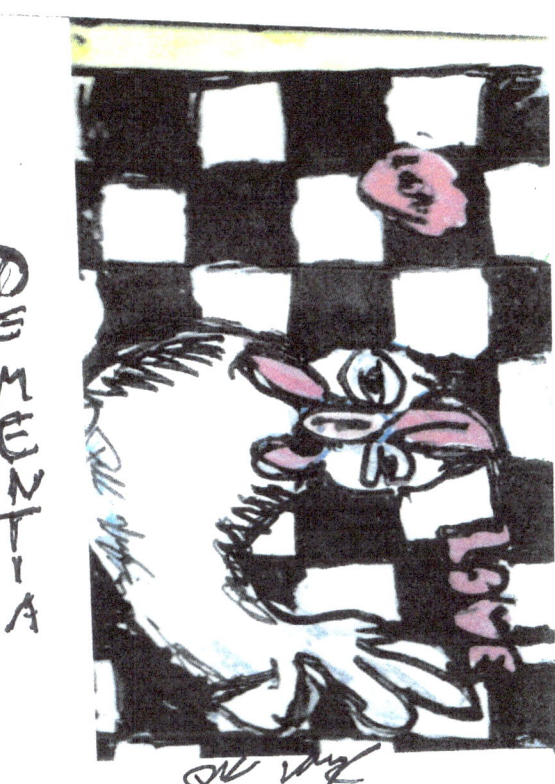

                    are we ever in control
who wins                who loses

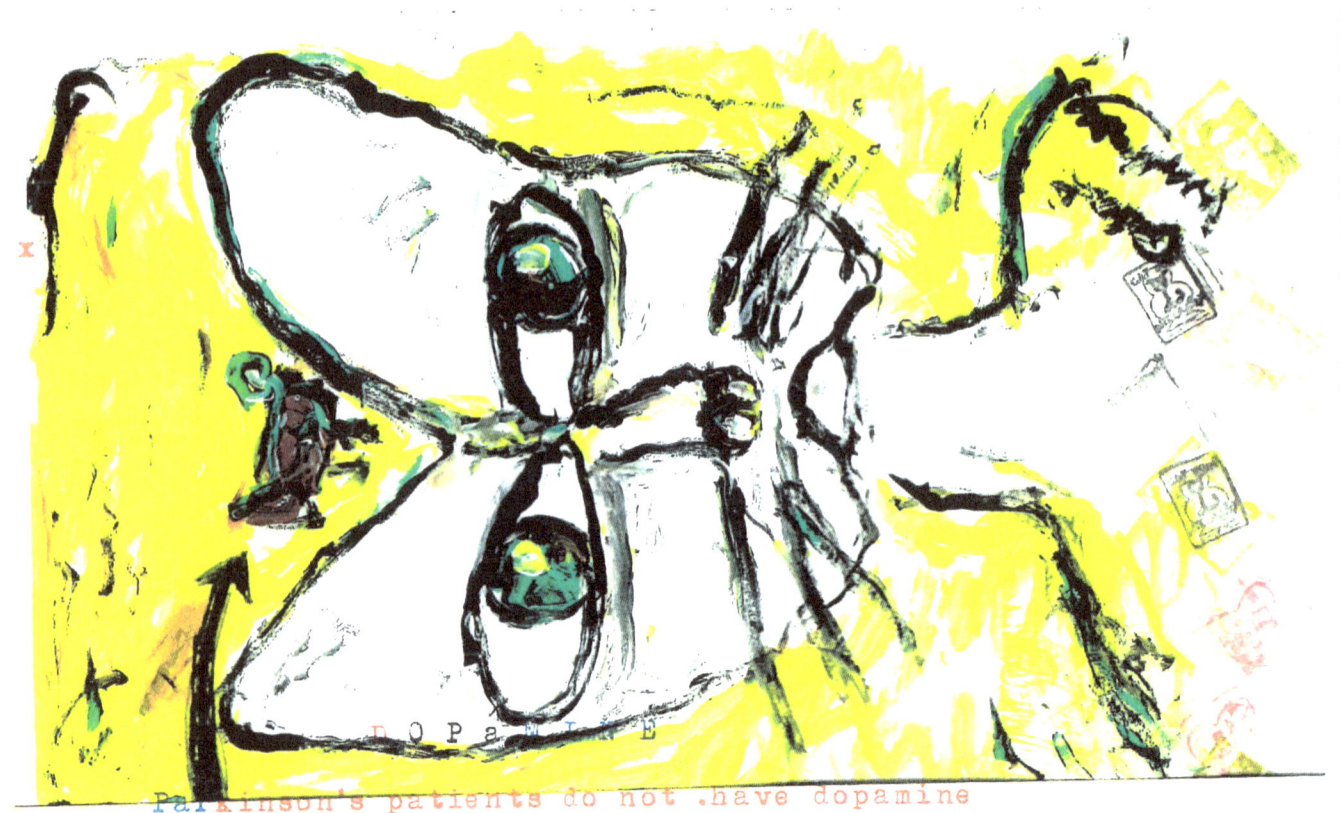

Parkinson's patients do not .have dopamine

travel to the  brain . they are like  an

unruly cat  that does not want to go , no

she does not want to go. with medicines like
  carbidopa , and levodopa you can feel normal

what is normal who is normal

DOPAMINE, O' DOPAMINE
be "m.ne"

do you want to be normal

who decides            conspiracy to
  know the truth
  , , mm   ,,,,,m        can  o move

need dopamine  have dopamine will travel

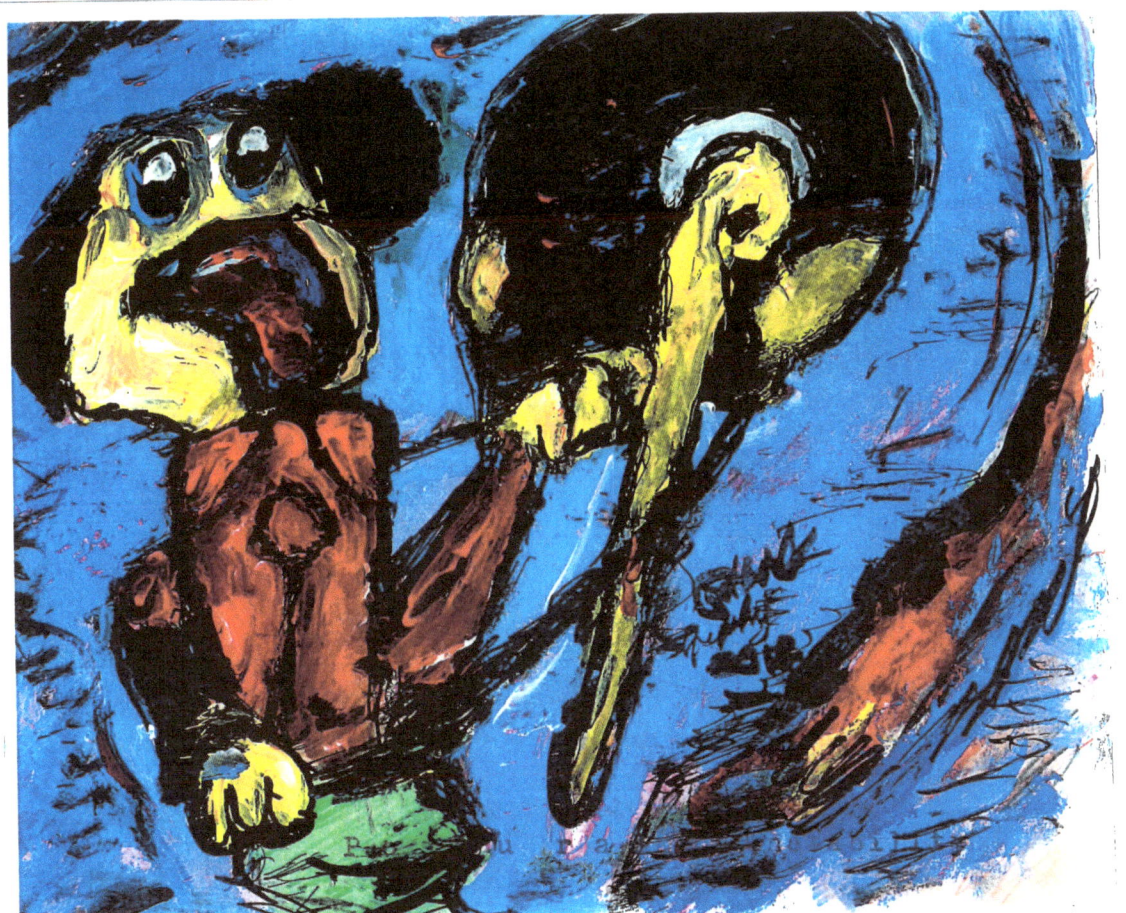

no longer in control      feel like a mouse

# POSTURAL INSTABILITY

a M ouse riding a    bicycle broken an accident

a betrayal of my limbs    why can i not move

crash crash        boom boom will i
                        break

all my bones           do i need a lawyer

VOICE

VOICE

YOUR        Voice beomes smaller

bb        shallow do not have a LOud voice                    ↓
          silent  x  X marks the spot,  spot can not

    Bark. yes he will bite, hear my voice

    make your voice be heard Shallow
        low voice     can you hear me

VOICE                    voice

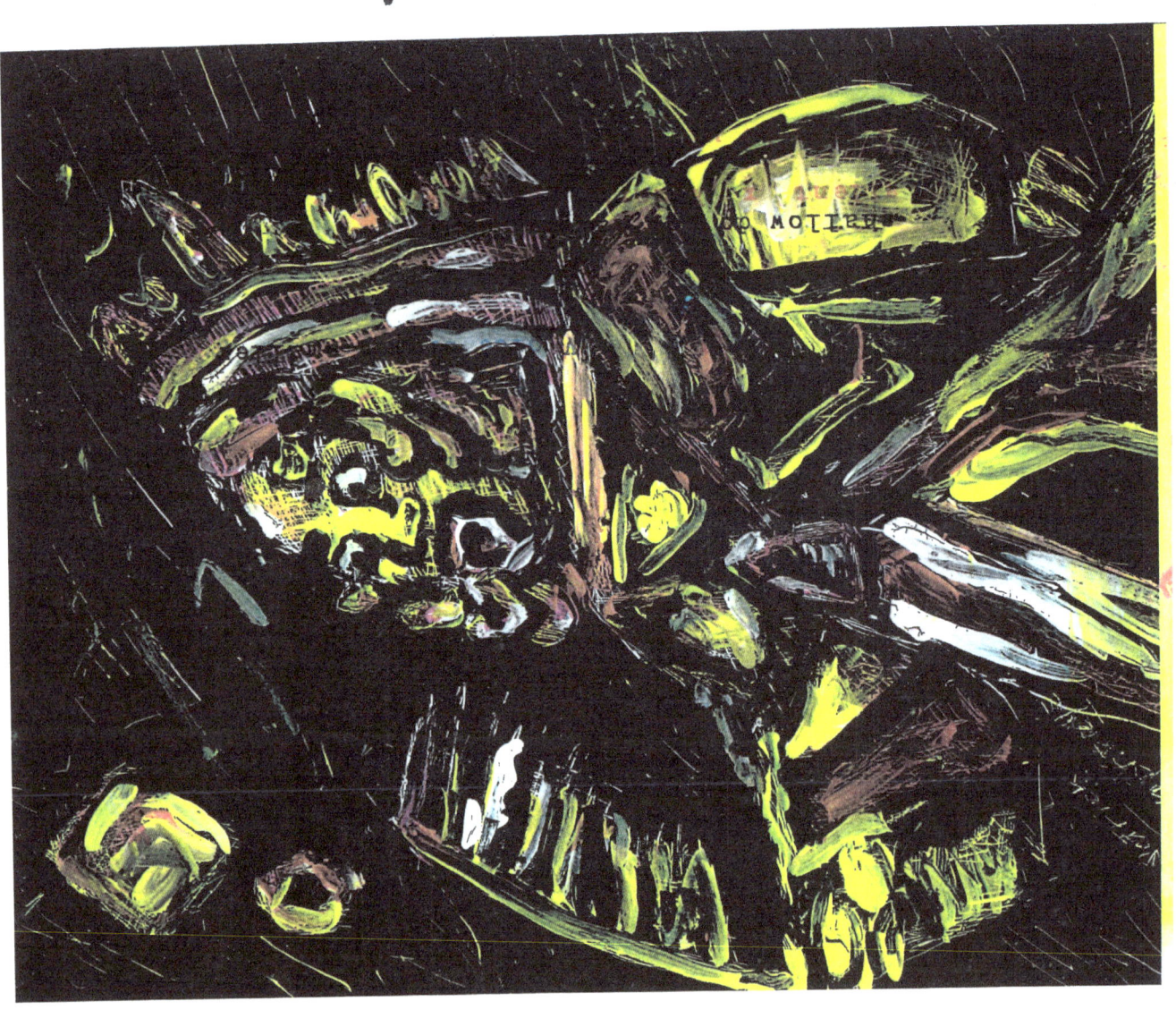

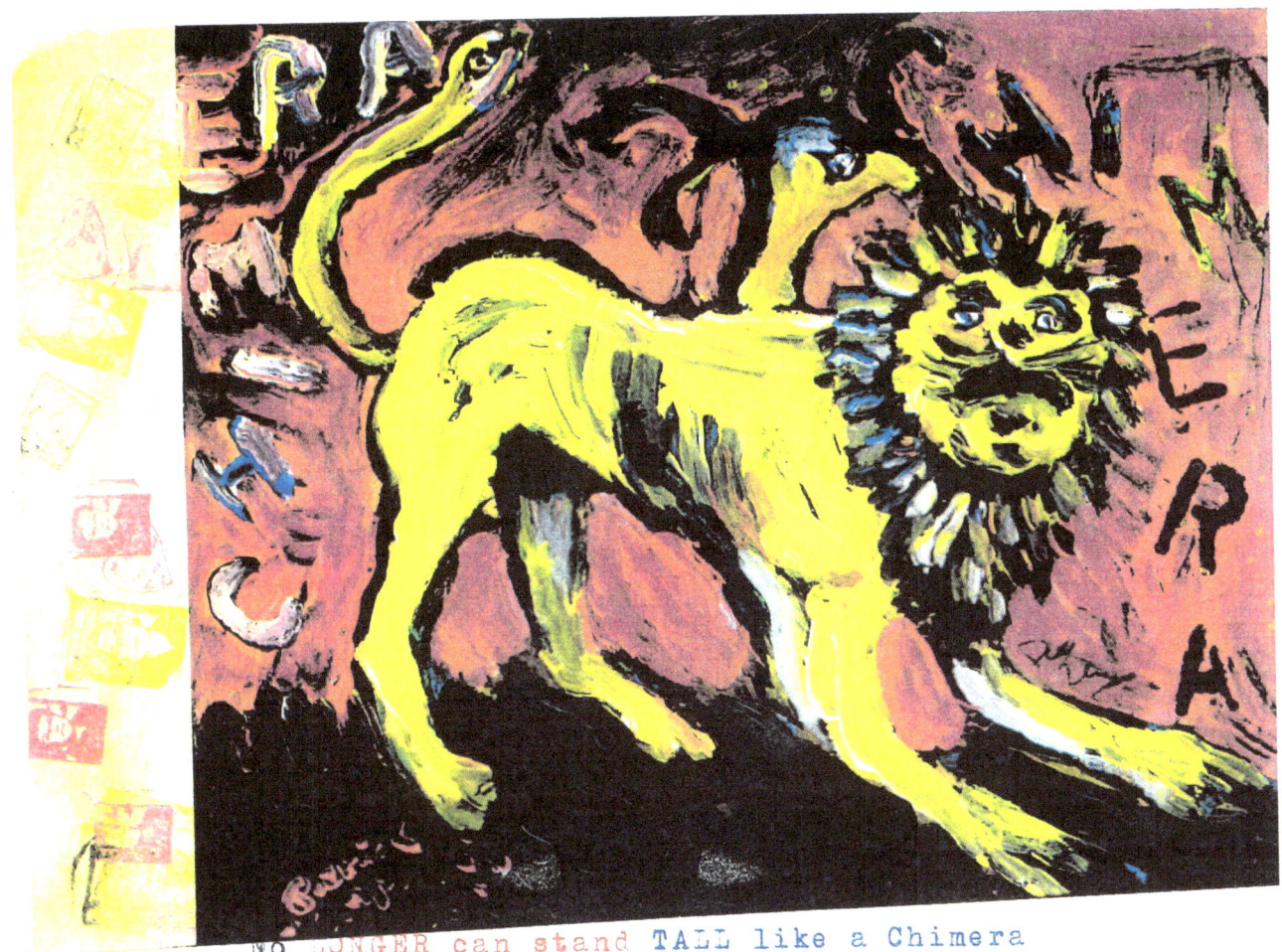

NO LONGER can stand TALL like a Chimera

I am Stooped over like an old Man

barely can move shuffle my feet  shuffle
      my resolve       will i make it there or
n     no where         do not pass go no $200


CHIMERA

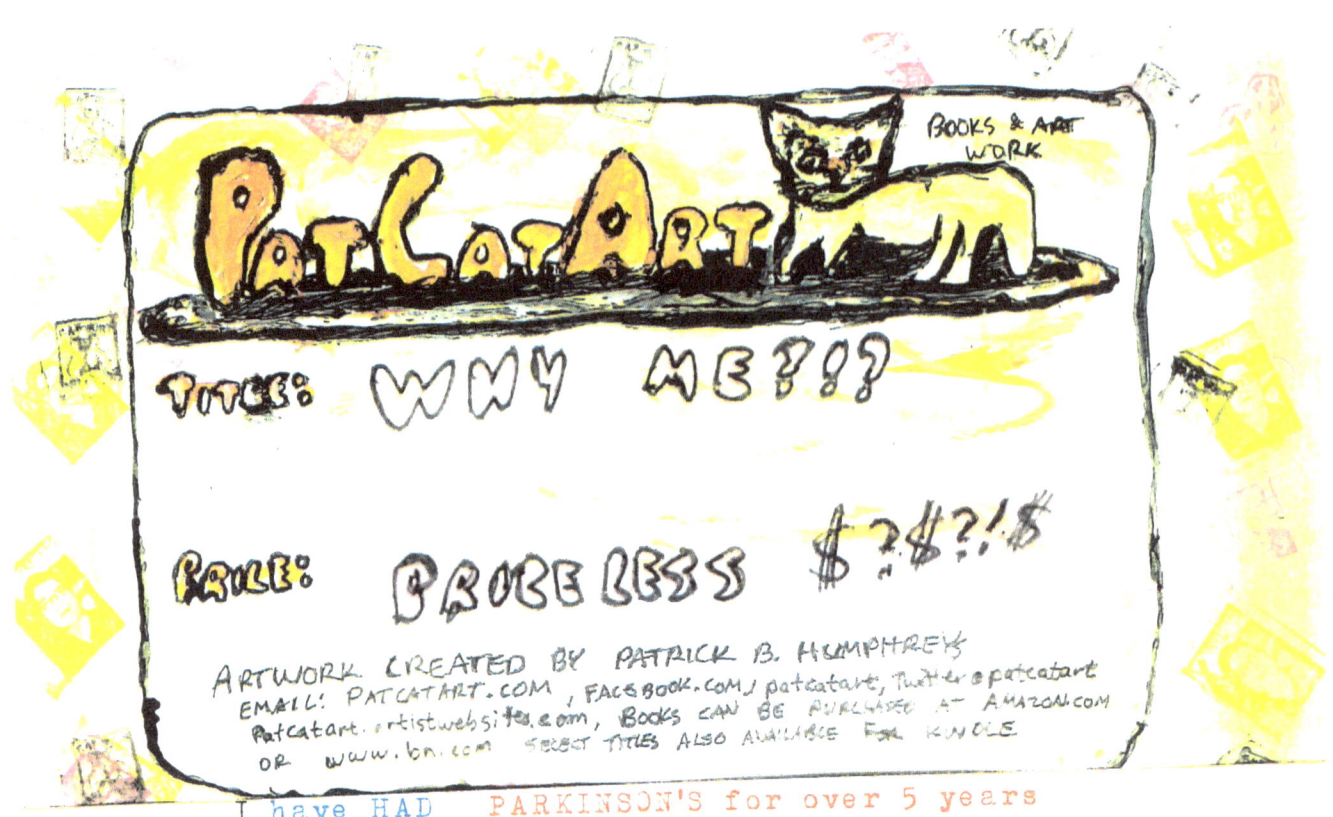

TITLE: WHY ME?!?

PRICE: PRICELESS $?$?!$

ARTWORK CREATED BY PATRICK B. HUMPHREYS
EMAIL: PATCATART.COM, FACEBOOK.COM/ patcatart, Twitter @patcatart
Patcatart.artistwebsites.com, BOOKS CAN BE PURCHASED AT AMAZON.COM
OR www.bn.com SELECT TITLES ALSO AVAILABLE FOR KINDLE

I have HAD    PARKINSON'S for over 5 years

          Why why    w    h    y    ?!?  @
          shaking so bad i could not  even
       si gn my name i was s h a k i n g shaking
          i   taught myself to draw and paint with my left
hand     now i can use both hands my work is stronger now


       better msrk making mark with right hsnd

       mark left     right wrong no better together



                    Pat Cat Art

R I G I D i T y

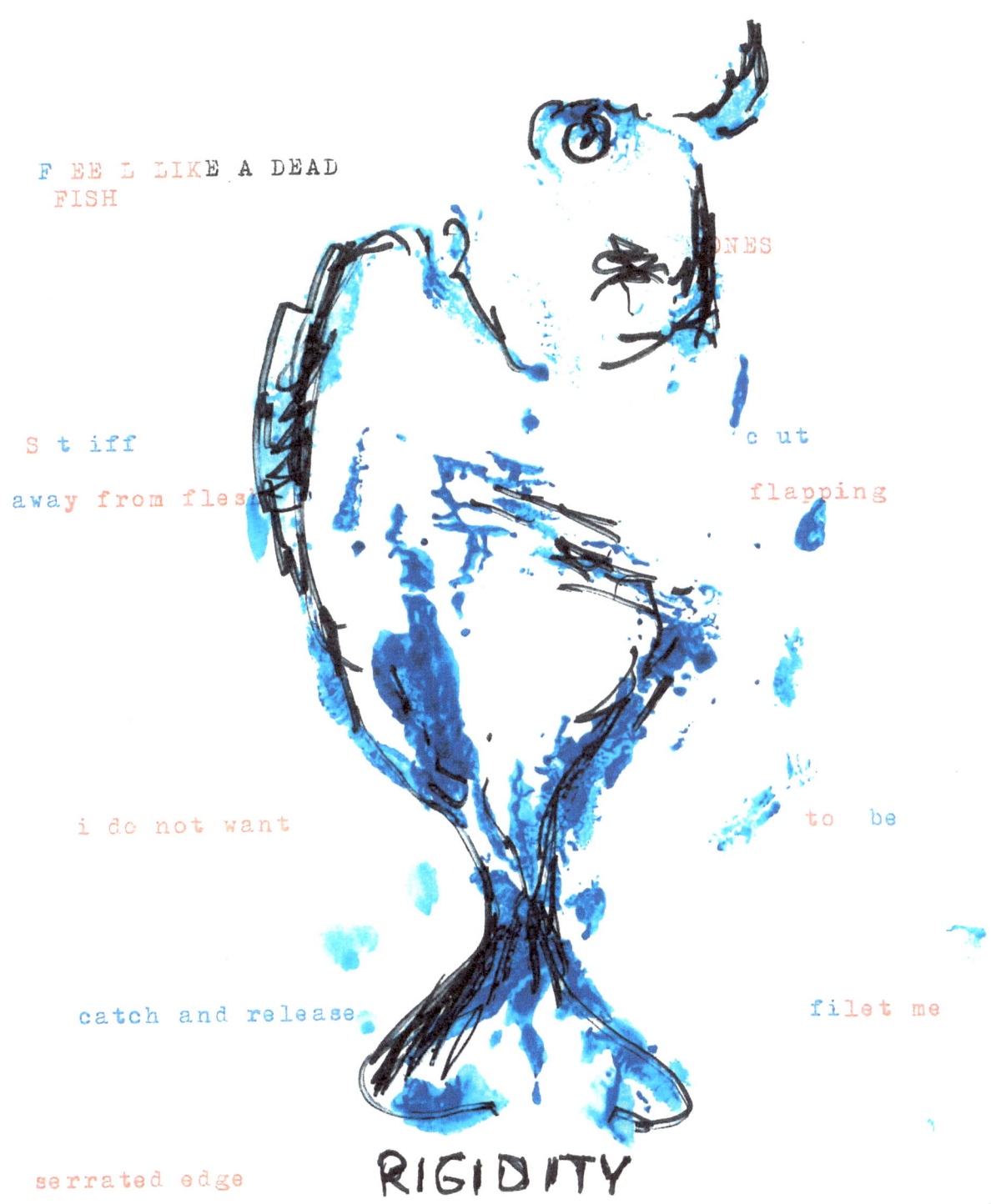

F EE L LIKE A DEAD
FISH

ONES

S t iff                                                              c ut

away from flesh                                                  flapping

i do not want                                                        to  be

catch and release                                                filet me

serrated edge                    RIGIDITY

SUNSET
SIDEWAYS

SIDEWAYS
SUNS3T

sU de waYS

red        yellows radiant blues

burni             put out the fire

kindling spreading the doubting my resolve

Not a goof  not a loser ,get  me to the

Sunday game will my team win

my bookie will hurt me if  i lo

JUMBLED

artist

with

parkinsons

# HOPE !!!

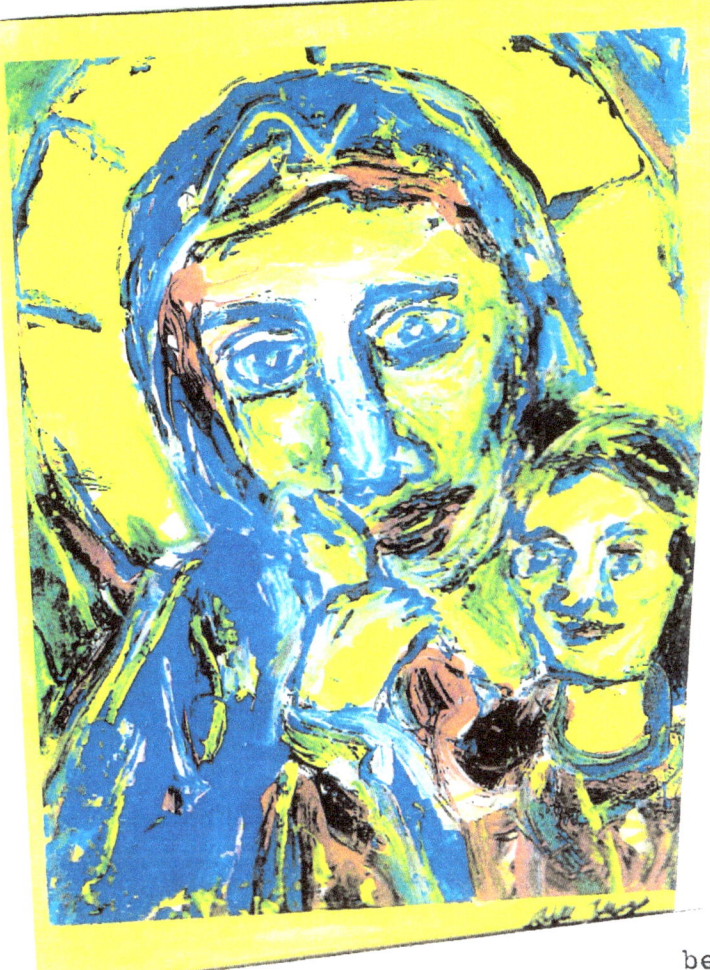

NeVER LOSE

do not let go

hold me

Mother please

i am your only

begotten Son

## ALWAYS HOPE !!!

never Lose Hope

there is always hope

pray for a cure for Parkinson's
There is always HOPE

PATCATART

ART OBJECTS

Patrick B. Murphy

BAY CITY MICHIGAN AND ONLINE: patcatart @gmail.com, patcatart.artistwebsites.com, twitter, and Facebook

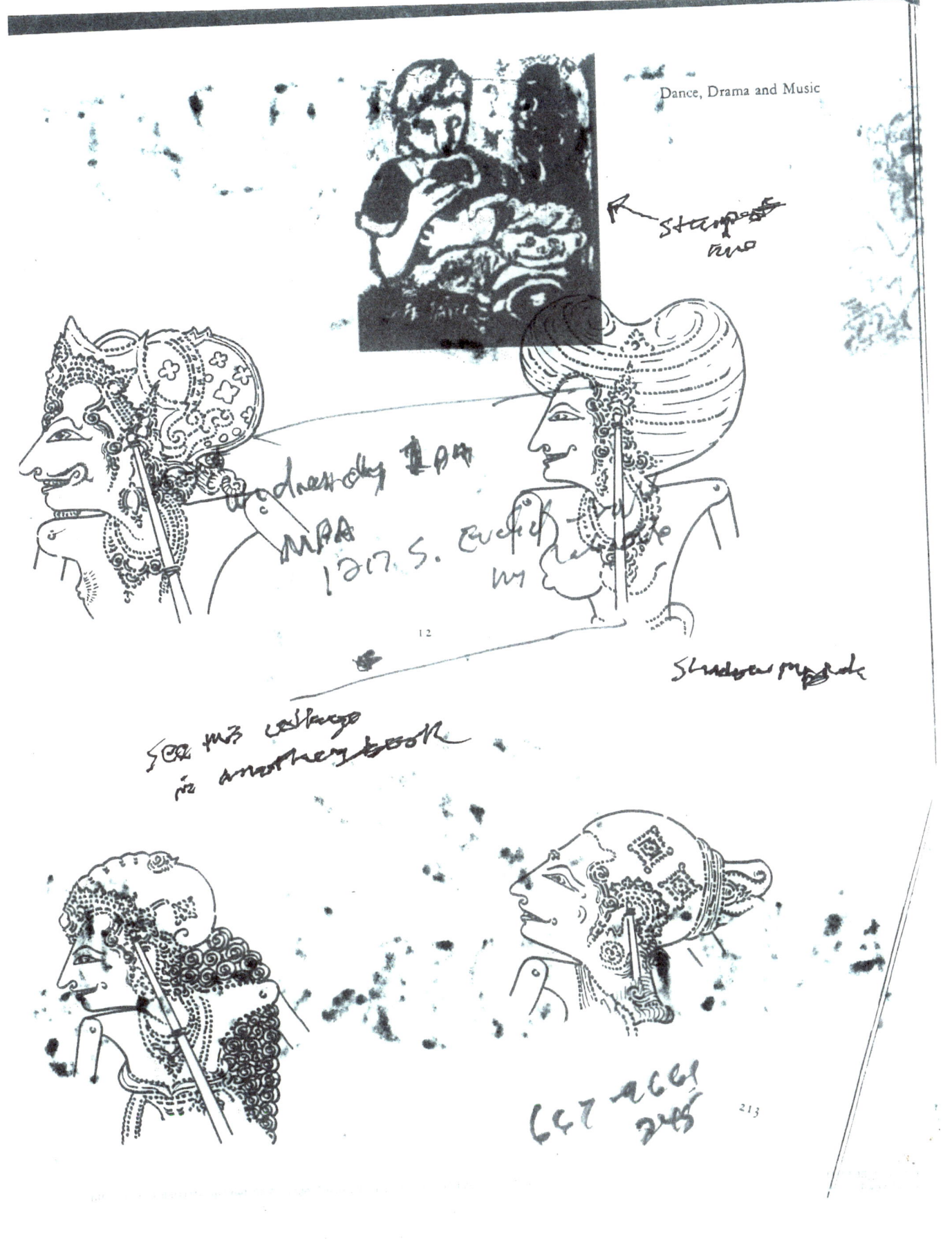

12

www.ingramcontent.com/pod-product-compliance
Lightning Source LLC
Chambersburg PA
CBHW050912180526
45159CB00007B/2891